B.S.

And Other Advice about Money

Disclaimer from Author
Not reading will make you illiterate (which means that you will be stupid). Reading this book may conjure up ideas and inspire you to take action. Here is the agreement; if you get filthy rich from ideas inspired by this book, then I won't ask you to share your good fortune with me. On the contrary, if you take risks and lose money, don't sue me. Agreed? Take responsibility for your actions. If you do strike it rich though, then I will let you buy me dinner. Any speiling errors ar Missis Teely's falt. Mi fith grade teecher said I wood never amount to any thing. Note to self: Don't ever pay attention to negative people who have never risked everything that they have for a dream. Enjoy.

Other Books by Woody Woodward

Your Emotional Fingerprint
7 Secrets That Will Transform Your Life

Millionaire Dropouts
Inspiring Stories of the World's Greatest Failures

Millionaire Dropouts
Biography Edition

Millionaire Dropouts
High School Edition

Millionaire Dropouts
Words of Wisdom

Millionaire Dropouts
Innovators

The Book of Riches
The 7 Secrets to Wealth

Conversations with Entrepreneurs

ACHIEVE
Conversations with Top Achievers

Entrepreneur on Fire
Conversations with Visionary Entrepreneurs

Entrepreneur on Fire
Conversations with Visionary Leaders

Dedication

To my mom
who taught me
everything that I know
about B.S.

"You are lying!" she yelled, as I followed her from room to room while she was cleaning up the house. The stories and excuses I gave her never satisfied her. After 30 minutes of ingenuous, Tom Sawyer quality excuses, my mom finally turned to me out of frustration and said, "That is B.S.!" Only being eleven years old, and not savvy to the adult world's system of abbreviations, I curiously asked my mom what B.S. stood for. She paused, and I could see this puzzling look come over her face as she chose her next words carefully. Finally, she pointed her finger and shouted, "It's your Belief System, now go to your room."

We are all full of our own B.S. (our own Belief Systems). Your Belief System will have the greatest impact on your life; it will have a greater effect on you than your family, your friends, or your profession. It is absolutely molded, twisted, stretched, and influenced by your family, friends, profession, and other external forces. The reality is that you and I are full of B.S. However, what you consciously choose to do with your B.S. makes all the difference.

This book is crafted to challenge your Belief System and to get you to think about what is possible for your life and for your business. Through more than 25 years of being an entrepreneur, business consultant, and researcher of human behavior, I often get the question, "How can I make more money?" The following anecdotes are designed to answer that question for you.

A long time ago, two brothers came to America to sell shoes. One brother wrote to the other, "We're out of luck! Indians don't wear shoes. This is a horrible turn of fate! Who will buy my stock of shoes?" The second brother saw the situation differently. He replied to his brother, "Great! Indians don't wear shoes! Don't you realize what an opportunity we have?" The same situation could be viewed as an amazing opportunity or as a horrible problem. You need to ask yourself, "What is the difference between the two brothers?" It was their Belief Systems. It was the way that they thought as well as their perceptions about their opportunities. How we go about defending and supporting our B.S. determines whether we fail or succeed in our lives, our relationships, and our business endeavors.

When striving to make money, your Belief System and the following five principles will increase your odds of creating revenue for yourself and for your business. In order to be successful, you need to adhere to the five principles of Mindset, Opportunities, Networking, Entrepreneurship, and being Yourself (M.O.N.E.Y.).

M.O.N.E.Y.

"M" = Mindset

The Landlord's Game vs. Monopoly

When an employer tells you, "You're fired," those words stir up emotions of anger, fear, self-doubt, anxiety, and so much more. For those of us who have been fired, we still remember where we were standing when we got the news. It is life changing. During the height of the Great Depression, Charles Darrow had a similar experience when he was fired from his job. Barely able to make ends meet, he, his pregnant wife, and his small child lived in a rundown, old house in Germantown, Pennsylvania. He would try to find odd jobs mowing lawns or doing manual labor. Times were hard and he competed with other unemployed men for the simplest of jobs. He knew that he had to do something different in order to provide for his family. To pass the time, in the evenings, his friends would play a homemade game where you would buy and sell real estate.

For the past 30 years, there had been many such games, including the original The Landlord's Game that was invented by Elizabeth (Lizzie) Maggie in 1904. She had patented the board game that same year. In 1910, she presented the game to George Parker of Parker Brothers and she was turned down. Her first games were handmade and they sold poorly. However, people who played the game started making their own versions that were based on Lizzie's invention. In 1924, Lizzie patented the game again after her first patent expired. She made some subtle changes to the names of the streets and she introduced a "Monopoly" card. Once again, Lizzie presented the game to Parker Brothers and she was turned away for a second time.

From 1924 to 1933, other enterprising individuals had created similar games, including Dan Layman, who sold his version under the name Finance, Rudy Copeland, who created Inflation, and Louis and Fred Thun, who saw Maggie's patent, and then decided to copyright their changes to the Monopoly game, as well.

The game that Darrow had played in 1933 was a knockoff version of Lizzie's. He became so enamored by the game that he started making his own version by using linoleum flooring for the board. He used paint samples from the local hardware store to give each property its own color. And, he carved game pieces from scraps of wood. It would take him an entire day to make one game board and pieces. His friends started requesting a copy of the game, and because he was unemployed, and had some free time, he obliged. He made some changes from the original one, such as changing some names of the properties as well as the layout of the board. Eventually, other people started requesting him to make one for them, as well. He ended up patenting his version of the game.

By now, he was in the heart of the Depression, and by anyone's standards, it probably would not have been a good time to start a company. On May 31, 1934, Darrow pitched his version to Milton Bradley, and he was turned down. Undaunted, he took it to Parker Brothers, who on October 19, 1934 not only turned it down, but they also wrote a personal note explaining the 52 reasons why the game was not a good idea as well as spelling out in great detail why they thought that it would never sell in the current consumer market. And, here is where history was made, because Darrow could have given up like Lizzie, and he could have just assumed that it wasn't going to sell. He had 52 reasons from the "experts" outlining why his version was not a marketable idea. Competition was rampant with others who were making their own versions of this game. It isn't difficult to imagine the conversation that he must have had with his wife, who now had two small children, when he told her the news that he wanted to be an entrepreneur. Given his situation, how could he ever hope to justify asking his wife for permission to borrow money from people and to embark upon a highly unrealistic profession of making his own games? His determination to not give up, his ability to think differently from the "experts" of the day, and the fact that he was internally driven was what enabled him to change history. How many entrepreneurs, business professionals, and landlords got their first taste of business from playing Monopoly®? Sure, he may not have found a vaccination for Polio or ended world hunger, but every person on this planet has the ability to change history in some small way by their very actions. Through perseverance, Darrow pulled together enough money to have 5,000 copies made. He started selling his board game on street corners. As people played it and shared it with their friends, game orders started coming in. He literally was getting orders from around the country, even though he was not advertising his board game. It wasn't long until one department store in Philadelphia ordered 5,000 copies.

The Parker Brothers (George and Charles) got wind of this surprising success. After seeing the success Darrow created for himself they had a change of heart and ended up licensing Darrow's patent. They paid him a royalty on every game of Monopoly, which made him a multi-millionaire. According to the book, The Monopolization of Monopoly by Burton H. Wolfe, Parker Brothers took several precautions in order to protect their investment:

Parker Brothers bought Lizzie Maggie's game for $500 (with no royalties). And, they made a promise to manufacture The Landlord's Game under its original title without changing any of the rules. Parker Brothers marketed a few hundred sets of The Landlord's Game, and then stopped. Lizzie was not interested in profiting from the game, but she was happy that a major company had finally consented to distribute it.

Parker Brothers bought Finance for $10,000 from David W. Knapp, who had bought the game from cash-strapped Dan Layman for $200. The company simplified the game, and then continued to produce it for a couple of years.

In the spring of 1935, Parker Brothers paid Luis Thun a visit. And, they offered to buy any remaining versions of the Monopoly game for $50 each.

Early in 1936, Parker Brothers sued Rudy Copeland for patent infringement on a game that Copeland had made, Inflation. Copeland countersued by charging that Darrow's patent, and therefore Parker Brothers' patent on Monopoly, was invalid. The case was settled out of court. Parker Brothers bought the rights to

Copeland's Inflation for $10,000, which was the same fee that they had paid for Finance.

What was the primary difference amongst these five people: Lizzie Maggie, David Knapp, Luis Thun, Rudy Copeland, and Charles Darrow? It was their mindset; their Belief Systems were radically different. Darrow's Belief System (B.S.) was unique in that even though it was the Great Depression, he was not willing to quit or back down. None of these designers and inventors were educated, toy industry professionals. They didn't come from a family of money. Multiple people had presented the game to Parker Brothers on many different occasions, throughout several decades, and they had all been rejected. The difference is that Darrow had a different mindset. Even though it was the Great Depression, he was willing to take a calculated risk and to sell his version of Monopoly on street corners. This resolve led to orders, word of mouth, and eventually the attention of Parker Brothers. He did not give up when it wasn't working, but rather he took massive action to create the future that he wanted for himself and for his family.

Determination, drive, fearlessness, innovation, and inspiration all come from having a positive mindset. When you have the courage to press forward when the "experts" say that it is not a good idea, then you have the opportunity to create your own future.

How to Change Your Mindset

Guard Your Thoughts:

The way that you think is projected through every fiber of your being, and it creates your perspective, vision, doubts, and fears. One day, my oldest son Hunter was talking about how he loved horses. So, as a family, we drove about 30 minutes to a horse training facility to sign him up for riding lessons. While I was watching him in the arena his instructor told him to drop the reins, sit up straight, and look to his left. All of the sudden, this 1,800 pound majestic horse was being magically steered by a 4 foot tall, 60 pound kid, without pulling on the reins. Fascinated, I had to inquire how this was possible. The instructor told me, "Depending on where you focus, your entire body responds. If you look to the left, then your shoulders, head, waist, and legs all move in that direction. The horse can feel your every movement, and it will turn accordingly." This is the same thing that we get in our own lives. When we change our focus by changing our thoughts, then our entire body, mood, and behavior changes and we can accomplish our purpose.

James Allen, in his classic book, *As a Man Thinketh*, wrote, "Let a man radically alter his thoughts, and he will be astonished at the rapid transformation it will effect in the material conditions of his life. Men imagine that thought can be kept secret, but it cannot; it rapidly crystallizes into habit, and habit solidifies into circumstances."

The key word here is "radically." If you don't like your situation, then you should radically alter your thoughts to create a new focus and a new perspective. The way that you radically alter your thoughts is by choosing something else to focus on. When a negative thought comes into your mind, then you should consciously replace it, and actively pursue a more uplifting thought. You will never rise higher than your thoughts. That is why you must vigilantly guard and protect them.

You should always guard your thoughts by reevaluating the music you listen to, the movies you watch, the websites you visit, and the conversations you participate in to achieve your optimal mindset.

Change Your Perspective:

One day, my youngest son Pierce (who was 5 years old at the time) was playing doubles tennis on the Nintendo® Wii by himself. He was using two joysticks, and thus playing both sides simultaneously. I overheard him getting really mad and complaining about how he couldn't win. As I saw what was going on, it took everything I had not to laugh. I explained to him that one team is always going to win and one team is always going to lose. And, because he was playing both teams at the same time, he was both winning and losing simultaneously. But, he was determined to win. He played about six more games, and then out of frustration he said, "I quit, I can never win!" He visualized that he wasn't winning. Therefore, he internalized failure and he just gave up. How many of us do this same thing with our lives? Something bad happens, we get frustrated, we become angered about our situation, and then we just give up when in reality we need to change our perspective. In order to change your perspective, you should commit to being determined and to changing your focus. If you do this, then you will change your outcome.

Some of the best research ever conducted on the power of thought was published in 1958 by L. Verdelle Clark in his thesis for Wayne State University. His research paper, "The effect of mental practice on the development of a certain motor skill" can be summarized as:

At the University of Chicago, a study was conducted to determine the effects of visualization on the free-throw performance of basketball players. First, the athletes were tested to determine their free-throw proficiency. They were then randomly assigned to one of three experimental groups. The first went to the gym every day for one hour and practiced throwing free throws. The second group also went to the gym, but instead of physically practicing, they lay down and simply visualized themselves successfully shooting. The third group did nothing. In fact, they were instructed to forget about basketball: "Don't touch a basketball—don't even think about it!" At the end of 30 days, the three groups were again tested to determine their free-throw proficiency.

The players who hadn't practiced at all showed no improvement in performance; many in that group actually exhibited a drop. Those who had physically practiced one hour each day showed a performance increase of 24 percent. Here's the clincher, the visualization group, by merely imagining themselves successfully shooting free throws, improved 23 percent!

This is quite significant. We can no longer ignore the fact that our thoughts and the way that we visualize performance have a significant impact on our outcomes. To change your perspective and outcome, you should pay attention to what you focus on, what you visualize, and what you think about. We must change our negative, self-loathing, self-pitying external thoughts to optimistic, conscious, encouraging internal thoughts if we want to solve our problems.

Examples of People Who Had a Positive Mindset:

J.K. Rowling's first publication of Harry Potter and the Sorcerer's Stone was 1,000 books. No one could have anticipated the worldwide success of her little story of a wizard and his friends. In 2008, the Harry Potter series had sold between 400-450 million copies.

When Bell telephone was struggling to get started, its owners offered all their rights to Western Union for $100,000. The offer was disdainfully rejected with the pronouncement, "What use could this company make of an electrical toy." Out of the world's estimated 7 billion people, 6 billion have access to mobile phones. However, if you add landlines to this equation, then there are more phones than there are people.

An expert said of football legend Vince Lombardi, "He possesses minimal football knowledge and he lacks motivation." Lombardi would later write, "It's not whether you get knocked down; it's whether you get back up."

Erik Weihenmayer climbed Mt. Everest, the tallest mountain in the world, on May 25, 2001. His feat was different from most people's experiences of climbing the mountain because he is blind.

Joyce Hall, founder of Hallmark, received a phone call that said his entire inventory had gone up in a fire 2 weeks before Valentine's Day. He did not have enough insurance to cover his debt or to reorder more inventory. Within 24 hours, he and his brother secured their own printing press, and they started making their own designs and cards.

How to Guard Your Thoughts and to Change Your Perspective:

1. **Gratitude Experiment:** For 7 days, write down 50 unique things you are grateful for. At the end of the week, you will have identified 350 unique things you feel grateful for which will change your perspective.

2. **Random Acts of Kindness:** Buy someone's meal, coffee, gas, or groceries. Take flowers to a widow. Make sandwiches and take them to the homeless shelter.

3. **Media Fast:** For 7 days (or 30 days if you are feeling brave), don't watch TV, movies, or play games on any electronic devices. You will be shocked at how much extra time you have to think.

4. **Read Biographies:** Go to the library. In the children's section, they have short biographies of almost anyone that you want to know about. Going to the children's section will save you time and you can read multiple bios.

5. **Read:** One suggestion is to read As A Man Thinketh by James Allen. Undoubtedly, it is one of greatest books written on the power of thought. If you have already read it, I encourage you to read it again.

M.O.N.E.Y.

"O" = Opportunity

Friends and Foreigners

The two friends watched as jackrabbits scattered before them, while they drove past the city limits on a dirt road leading to open fields that were spotted with horses and orchards. Walter pulled the car over, and he vividly described what he was going to build on this desolate land to his friend, Arthur. He wanted to convince his friend to buy all the surrounding acreage. Walter told Arthur, "I can handle the main project myself. It will take all my money, but I want you to have the first chance at this surrounding acreage, because in the next 5 years it will increase in value several times." Arthur looked around and he thought to himself, "Who in the world is going to drive 25 miles for this crazy project? His dream has gotten the best of his commonsense." Arthur gave Walter all the excuses that a good friend could give while trying not to squash the other person's dream. Walter continued to implore Arthur to buy the remaining land, but Arthur would not concede. He gave a few more excuses about how money was a little tight, and that now was not the best time to invest, but he said that he would think about it and get back to Walter, who cautioned, "Later on will be too late. You had better move on it right now."

But, Art Linkletter failed to see the vision of his close friend Walt Disney. One year later, on July 18, 1955, Art was the master of ceremonies when Walt opened Disneyland. Art had missed out on the opportunity of a lifetime by failing to purchase the land surrounding one of today's most well-known amusement parks.

Walt's mind was set on building Disneyland. He even cashed in his life insurance policy to raise the necessary money to build his dream. However, Art's mindset was that the opportunity was too risky. He justified this feeling by claiming money was too tight. And frankly, he didn't feel Walt's vision would work, and so he passed on the opportunity. Within less than 8 weeks of Disneyland's opening, the theme park greeted its one millionth visitor. In 1954, the year Walt Disney was building his dream, the Fujishige family had a different mindset; they envisioned what the land could become. So, they purchased 56 acres of strawberry fields across the street from Disneyland for $10,000. In the late 1990's, the Disney Corporation paid the family just under a $100 million for the land.

An opportunity is an opportunity regardless whether friends or foreigners buy into it. At some point, you will likely have friends who will pass on opportunities that you present. And, I am not defining foreigners in the traditional sense of the word. A foreigner is someone who is foreign to you, and who is not in your inner circle of influence. Too often, the value we put on an opportunity is directly related to the approval of our inner circle of friends and family. When Walt was building Disneyland, everyone, including his brother and business partner Roy, did not believe in his concept for a family theme park. Over time, both his friends as well as people foreign to him saw his vision, and many bought into his opportunity.

Opportunities come and go, but a person with the right mindset has the potential to create an opportunity out of any situation.

Today's Problems are Tomorrow's Corporations

When Conrad was growing up, he wanted to be like his dad, a successful entrepreneur. His father owned many of the businesses in their small town. However, when his father found him sleeping in past 7:00 a.m. one day, he labeled him as a "lazy oaf who would never amount to anything." But, Conrad refused to believe that this label applied to him; he became very driven by working hard in school. He then entered politics. Conrad went on to win a seat in the state legislature of New Mexico. After serving 2 years in politics, he persuaded his father to open a bank with him. He started as a teller, and within a couple of years he worked his way from this entry level position to becoming bank president. Upon becoming president of the bank, he sought the opportunity to buy the bank from his father. His father refused. Conrad wanted to break out on his own, and so he looked for a different bank to buy. He had enough connections in the industry to borrow the money. Plus, he had saved some money of his own. After barely missing two opportunities to buy a small bank, he went to Cisco,

Texas where a banker was selling his bank. Conrad did not negotiate the price because he had already been out-bid twice before. The seller took his speedy offer as an impression that he might have been selling it for too little. The seller quickly raised the price, which frustrated Conrad. He went to the local hotel to find a room. Upon watching the bustling lobby, where there were more people than rooms, he asked the owner about his business. The owner acknowledged his business was healthy, but what he really wanted to do was to try his hand at the oil business. After talking for a little while and checking the hotel's financials, Conrad Hilton offered to buy the hotel. By the end of the day, Hilton was the proud owner of his first hotel.

He could have focused on the label that his dad had put upon him. He could have given up when he did not have the opportunity to buy the bank from his father. However, even though he was out to buy a bank, he had the right mindset to notice a good opportunity when he saw one. When the opportunity arose, he was prepared to meet the challenge. Today's problems can be tomorrow's corporations.

Examples of Companies That Were Started by High School/College Dropouts:

According to the U.S. Department of Education, almost 10% of high school students drop out. They are considered not qualified for 90% of the jobs that are offered in the United States. They will make, on average, $260,000 less than a high school graduate, and roughly one million dollars less than a college graduate in their lifetime. With these staggering statistics, here is a list of 40 high school and college dropouts who have created their own opportunities regardless of their limited education.

"Always bear in mind that your own resolution to succeed is more important than any other."
—Abraham Lincoln

Dov Charney, founder of American Apparel

Amadeo Giannini, founder of Bank of America

Ben Cohen, founder of Ben & Jerry's Homemade Ice Cream

William Boeing, founder of The Boeing Company

Asa Candler, founder of The Coca Cola Company

Harry Cohen, founder of Columbia Pictures Industries, Inc.

Rick Rubin, founder of Def Jam Recordings

Michael Dell, founder of Dell Inc.

Tom Monaghan, founder of Domino's Pizza L.L.C.

Charles Dow, founder of Dow Jones & Company, Inc.

David Geffen and Steven Spielberg, co-founders of DreamWorks SKG

Florence Graham, founder of Elizabeth Arden, Inc.

Henry Ford, founder of Ford Motor Company

King Gillette, founder of The Gillette Company

Milton Hershey, founder of The Hershey Company

Kemmons Wilson, founder of Holiday Inn

Soichiro Honda, founder of Honda Automotive

David Neeleman, founder of JetBlue Airways

Jimmy Dean, founder of Jimmy Dean Foods

Colonel Sanders, founder of Kentucky Fried Chicken

Marcus Loew, founder of Loews Theatres

William Lear, founder of Lear Jets

Ole Kirk Christian, founder of Lego

Frank Mars, founder of Mars Candies

Ruth Handler, founder of Mattel Corp

Ray Kroc, founder of McDonald's Corporation

Bill Gates, founder of Microsoft Corporation

Berry Gordy, founder of Motown Records

David Sarnoff, founder of NBC

Larry Ellison, founder of Oracle

Patrick Frawley, founder of Paper Mate Pens

Ralph Lauren, founder of Polo and the Ralph Lauren Corporation

James Gamble, founder of Proctor & Gamble

Jann Wenner, founder of Rolling Stone Magazine

Frederick Royce, founder of Rolls-Royce Limited

Vidal Sassoon, founder of Vidal Sassoon Hair Products

Sir Richard Branson, founder of Virgin Enterprises, Ltd.

Dave Thomas, founder of Wendy's International, Inc.

John Mackey, founder of Whole Foods Market

How to Create Opportunities:

1. **Start Close to Home:** Define your strengths, talents, and expertise. Create a niche for yourself.

2. **Obey the Law of Reciprocity:** You have to give to receive. Reach out to other people and see how you can help them. As you give service, you will discover available opportunities.

3. **Create a Plan:** If you fail to plan, then you plan to fail. What is your plan? Where do you want to be in the next 1, 5, and 10 years?

4. **Be Flexible:** Even though you have a plan, you should remain flexible. If you take an opportunity that is not 100% what you want, then it may lead to a better opportunity down the road. For example, Conrad Hilton went from wanting to own banks to being a hotel baron.

5. **Keep Your Eyes Open:** Even if your current opportunities are thriving, you should still take notice of what is on the horizon.

M.O.N.E.Y.

"N" = Networking

Lamborghinis and Ferraris

The V12 from Eddie Van Halen's Lamborghini filled the streets of Los Angeles, as he pulled into Claudio Zampolli's shop. Eddie noticed a cherry red Ferrari 512 Boxer on display in the showroom. Shop owner Zampolli said that it belonged to Sammy Hagar. And, he asked Eddie if he wanted to meet him. The band, Van Halen, which had just separated ways with their lead singer, David Lee Roth, was in need of a new front man. So, Eddie called Hagar from the shop phone.

The two knew each other slightly. About 10 years younger than Hagar, Eddie had been a huge fan of Montrose (Hagar's previous band) as a kid. He was not the type of man to waste time with small talk. So, Eddie asked Hagar if he wanted to be in Van Halen, and do a record with them.

Hagar had never liked the group, really. He liked Eddie's guitar playing, but he thought Roth's raunchy, larger-than-life persona was phony and repetitive. Hagar didn't want to be in someone else's band again.

Hagar flew to L.A. for a meeting with the Van Halen brothers. The three men went into Eddie's garage and they started jamming; the brothers started playing a riff on guitar and drums while Hagar made up the lyrics. They wrote two songs right there on the spot. The next morning, Hagar called and said, "I'm in."

Prior to Hagar, Van Halen had never had a #1 album. However, each of the four albums that Hagar and Van Halen did went straight to #1 status, and they ended up selling millions of copies. With their newfound wealth, from each of their albums, where do you think that they went to buy their next cars? They went to Claudio Zampolli.

When you network, you do not have to have an immediate benefit. Networking is not handing 10 business cards out to an acquaintance and saying, "Here are some cards for you and your friends." I have had this happen to me countless times. I always end up throwing them all away, including the one that was actually intended for me. Networking is about solving problems for people; it is not about promoting yourself. The fastest way to promote yourself is to solve someone else's problem. They will forever remember you, and they will typically refer you to their inner circle.

Relationships to Riches™

Before Chris Cortazzo became the #1 Real Estate Agent in Malibu, and, before he sold 1.8 billion dollars in real estate transactions, he was an assistant to celebrity photographer Herb Ritts. On one of Herb's shoots in Malibu, he was with actor Richard Gere. He heard Gere talking about how much he loved this certain house nearby. Chris said, "I just kayaked by it 3 days ago, and it is for sale for 5 million dollars." Later that week, Richard, his business manager, and Chris all met at the house, and Richard fell in love with it. So, he bought the home, and launched Chris' real estate career.

Cortazzo was from Malibu, and he was passionate about the area, but this information alone was not enough. He needed contacts, clients, potential sellers, and buyers. At first, these relationships came through his network with Herb Ritts. Through his relationships, people kept asking him, "Since you are from Malibu, where should I buy a house?" He was solving problems for people. These individuals started referring their friends and business partners to Cortazzo.

Where would Cortazzo be without his relationship with Ritts? Most likely, he would be a starving, new real estate agent, who would never have gone on to sell 1.8 billion dollars in transactions. Relationships are absolutely crucial to success. However, you have to add value to your network through selfless service and a disciplined work ethic.

Networking is defined as, "a supportive system of sharing information and services among individuals and groups that have a common interest."

Networking is NOT about self-promotion, talking about your accomplishments, making others feel small, or being the only person in the room with the right idea.

How to Network:

1. **Create Value for Others First:** What are their needs and how can you solve them?

2. **Branch Out:** Join a networking club. There are many in almost every city.

3. **Differentiate Yourself:** Be the best at something. What is your expertise?

4. **Follow Up:** Regularly reach out to your network, and see what you can do to add value.

5. **Be Concise:** Networking goes both ways. Know what you need so when someone asks you, "What do you need?" you have an answer. The worst thing you can say is "I am fine." What that means is they have no value to offer you.

Bonus: The Power of a Mastermind

Napoleon Hill's book *Think and Grow Rich* illustrates the power of a mastermind group. Hill was commissioned by Andrew Carnegie to interview 500 of the most influential and powerful people of the time on the subject of how they became successful in business. One of his discoveries was that all of them had belonged to some type of mastermind group.

Here is a list of techniques for how to conduct a mastermind group. These guidelines are not rules; they are just suggestions that work. You should create your own principles that work best for your industry.

- Mastermind groups typically consist of anywhere from 4-8 members.

- Meetings can range from monthly, bi-weekly, to weekly meetings, depending on need.

- Meetings can be in person or virtual.

- Members should have an equal amount of time to talk about their business.

- Transparency is necessary. No egos should be unchecked.

- However, the purpose can be to support each member in reaching their personal goals.

- One speaker can be the moderator. However, the moderator should switch each session.

- Each member should commit to an action.

- The following session, the moderator should hold everyone accountable to his or her previous commitments.

- Each member should give and receive support.

M.O.N.E.Y.

E = Entrepreneurship

The $30,000,000 Decision

By April of 2001, I had lost a net worth of over one million dollars. I was 27 years old, married, and I had a 6 month old son. Just a year earlier, the NASDAQ was at an all-time high of 5048. Within a year, it had dropped to 1700, signifying the Dot-com Bomb. Some billion dollar companies became non-existent overnight. We saw a sad tale of major corporations that lost 80% to 90% in valuation. (For example, Amazon went from $107 a share to $7 a share, while Cisco lost 87% valuation). Before this collapse, my small family had sold our business, and we had put our investments into the stock market.

After losing everything, we sold one house and we rented out the other, while we had to move into my parent's unfinished basement. As if the situation wasn't bad enough, I clearly remember the day my banker called and said, "Mr. Woodward, if we combine all of your accounts, it would equal $4.00. What would you like us to do?" All I could think was, "It wouldn't even buy my son a Happy Meal™."

We decided to start a new business in real estate. My wife started processing loans, and I went to obtain my real estate license. As my wife processed loans, I would deliver the checks, after closing from escrow, to the office of the broker that had originated the loan. I quickly noticed my wife was making $350 to $500 per transaction, while the broker was making $5,000 per loan on average. She was ordering the title documents, setting up escrow, getting appraisals, collecting the clients' information, and scheduling the closings. I asked her why the broker was making all of the money and she was doing all of the work. She said, "He originated the loan (which means that he found the client), and, therefore, he makes the bulk of the money." That day, I went down to city hall and I registered for a new business license as a mortgage broker. Learning the inner workings behind how mortgages are processed absolutely changed the projection of our lives. Within less than 6 months, we moved back into our home. Within 2 years, we were originating loans in seven states, and we were closing on $30,000,000 in transactions with 50 loan officers.

When you are learning the business behind the business you need to look for trends. The greatest place to search for trends is to look at history. History is a brilliant teacher; it tends to repeat itself. In 2005, the housing bubble was showing the same signs as the Dot-com Bomb. We decided to sell all of our investment properties, and we closed down our mortgage business. We were 2 years too early for getting out. Nevertheless, we got out at the height of the real estate market. Although I wish I could say I had the same impeccable timing with our other business ventures, we have not been as successful. However, an entrepreneur keeps getting up and keeps learning from his or her mistakes.

A Decade of Perseverance Pays Off

Rowland opened his first store in Boston the same year he was married. Within a short time, he and his new bride had to close their doors due to not knowing how to properly run a retail business. Undaunted, he quickly opened another store, which lasted only 2 years. By the age of 27, he went west to California to try his luck on a third store. He assumed a new location would remedy his situation. Within a year, this store also failed, and he packed his bags and moved back home. He was discouraged, but he refocused, and he set up a fourth store in Haverhill, Massachusetts, which went bankrupt within 2 years. When he was 36 years old, he was considered a massive failure by the world's standards. However, he thought differently from others, and he was determined to make his mark in retail. By learning from his many mistakes, he consulted experts on how to properly handle inventory, financing, shipping, employee training, and store layout. Rowland Macy opened his fifth store in New York City in 1858, which became the world's largest department store. The Macy's Department Store, which is located in Heralds Square in New York City, is still the world's largest department store, 156 years later.

Examples of Entrepreneurs
Who Learned the
Business Behind the Business:

Fred Smith, the founder of FedEx, was mocked by his college professor as he submitted his idea of overnight delivery for packages. After investing $22 million for planes, trucks, and distribution channels, his company only received 18 packages on its first day. However, he was undeterred. Today, FedEx ships over 10 million packages each day.

Ole Kirk Christiansen was losing so much money in his business that he turned to his family for financial help. They loaned him the money on one condition, "No more making toys." He ended up borrowing the money but kept making toys. He eventually changed the name of the company to LEGO.

Soichiro Honda was turned down by Toyota Motor Corporation during a job interview for an engineer position. He continued to be jobless until his neighbors started buying his "homemade scooters." Subsequently, he started his own company, the Honda

Motor Company. Today, the company has grown to become the world's largest motorcycle manufacturer. And, his company is more profitable than rival automakers, GM and Chrysler.

Akio Morita, the founder of Sony Corporation, had a failure for a first product, an electric rice cooker, which only sold 100 cookers (because it burned rice rather than cooking it). Today, Sony is generating $66 billion in revenue, and it is ranked as the world's sixth largest electronic company.

John Grisham's first novel was rejected by 16 agents and 12 publishing houses. Despite these rejections, he continued writing until he became best known as a novelist specializing in the genre of legal thrillers. The media has called him one of the best authors alive in the 21st century.

How to Know the Business Behind the Business:

1. **Mentorship:** One of the greatest mentorships of all time was between Anne Sullivan and Helen Keller. Keller was both deaf and blind, but through Sullivan's mentorship Keller became the first person to earn a Bachelor of Arts degree with a disability. Keller went on to become a lecturer as well as an activist for women's rights.

2. **Education:** You should always seek a higher learning to open your mind up to new possibilities. Albert Einstein said, "No problem can be solved from the same level of consciousness that created it."

3. **Watch for Signs:** Historical and economic events tend to repeat themselves. You should always look for trends and historical data to give you an edge in both business and in life. You should also remember the adage, "A lesson is repeated until it is learned."

4. **Form a Mastermind Group:** If you take a single, hot coal briquette and remove it from the other hot coal briquettes, then it will cool within 5 minutes. However, a group of briquettes will stay warm for hours. You should keep in mind the saying, "We are stronger together than we are separated." In a mastermind group, you will often find insights and solutions to your problems in business. You can join a mastermind group at www.ConnectToProfit.com.

5. **Innovate But Don't Duplicate:** You do not have to be first in your place of business, but the sooner you innovate, then the sooner you will separate yourself from the crowd. George Henry Lewes said, "No man ever made a great discovery without the exercise of the imagination." And, Einstein said, "Imagination is more important than knowledge." You should always attempt to exercise your imagination, and then you will often discover new ways to run your business.

M.O.N.E.Y.

Y = You

Dirty Pictures

"Be more concerned with your character than your
reputation, because your character is what you
really are, while your reputation is merely what
others think you are."   — John Wooden

In the 1960's, Walt Disney was reading in the paper one
day about what people thought about the cinema and
the modern trends. He came across a comment by Dick
Van Dyke where he said, "I personally did not like the
new trend. They are dirty pictures." Walt liked what
he had read and he felt the same way. So, he called in
Dick, and he asked him to come to the studio to read
for the part of Bert in the movie *Mary Poppins*. Prior to
his work in Mary Poppins, Dick Van Dyke had only
been in two small films. By having character and being
true to himself, Dick went on to have one of the longest
careers in Hollywood, which is a city that is notorious
for not celebrating residents that practice integrity

of character. He has been on television every decade since the 1950's, and he has been in 18 motion pictures. At age 88, he was still on the set with TV shows and movie projects in the works. His long, successful career makes one ask, "What is the price for being yourself?" Priceless.

The Midas Touch

"Character cannot be developed in ease and quiet. Only through experience of trial and suffering can the soul be strengthened, ambition inspired, and success achieved." —Helen Keller

Success came naturally to this person in the beginning, but what happened to him later proved his greatness. By the age of 8, he was selling excess vegetables from his mother's garden. By age 10, he upgraded from carrying them in a basket to pushing them in a wheelbarrow. He later increased his produce business again. And, by the age of 12, he was using a horse and cart. To further his success, he hired his siblings and his neighbors. By the age of 15, he ran a full-fledged produce business that was supplying local grocers.

His father took notice of his son's success, and he invited him to be part of the family's brick manufacturing business. As he became more involved in the company, he took some college courses, and by the age of 21, he had saved enough money to buy a half interest in the company.

When his parents returned from a long trip in Europe, they were shocked to find he had built them a lovely brick home. He used the bricks from their factory, and he paid the other contractors by collecting money that was owed to the company, which his father had given up on ever seeing.

At the age of 25, he partnered with L.C. Noble to produce and sell bottled pickles and horseradish sauce. He always had a passion for fresh produce, and there was a real need for bottled ready-to-use foods. People snatched up their products at breakneck speed, and within a very short period they took on a third partner to further expand their business. Everything he touched seemed to turn to gold.

Their company and product line grew. They expanded to a large warehouse, and added more product lines, including vinegar, sauerkraut, and celery sauce. Before his thirty-second birthday, however, everything would change. To take advantage of their growing business, this man and his partners signed contracts with large farmers to buy next year's crops at a fixed price. Unfortunately, this turned out to be a mistake. That year was a bumper crop, and the price for produce was driven down. However, the company had already contracted to pay a higher, fixed price.

Sadly, due to this miscalculation, he lost everything he had worked so hard to build. At the same time, there was a business panic, which affected the banks, and he could no longer procure a loan for his company. Even with borrowing from friends, family, and his own life insurance policy, there still was not enough money to keep the company afloat for more than a few months. In a sick twist of fate, he even lost the home he had built for his parents because he had put a lien against it in order to secure a loan for his business. In addition, he had legal problems. The authorities had arrested him twice for fraud, although he was proven innocent each time. Toward the end of this series of misfortunes, people he had done business with for years would not give him credit to buy food for his family. After the final shred of his reputation was sullied, he had no choice but to file for bankruptcy.

Never before had he been in such a dismal place with no hope of turning it around. A life that seemed to be a stepping stone from success to success was now dashed on the rocks of business failure. Furthermore, he was banned from being an entrepreneur. The terms of his bankruptcy barred him from owning any part of a company. Nevertheless, this man was undeterred. Relying on his creativity and his belief system, he convinced his cousin and his brother to start another food processing business in which he would be hired as a manager. Business drummed along in this manner until they were able to leverage an opportunity with one of their more profitable products, their ketchup line.

Through perseverance and indomitable spirit, this man was eventually discharged from his bankruptcy and he gained the respect of his creditors. Although he was not required to pay back his debts, he spent the next 13 years doing so. He also earned and saved enough money to buy his relatives' shares in the company.

This man never took his eyes from his goals, and he continued to build his business. Deciding that he needed a clever marketing campaign, he was inspired by an advertisement for "21 styles of shoes." He thought he needed some type of catchy slogan, like this one, to attract people to his products. For some reason, the number "57" seemed appropriate. So, Henry John Heinz started advertising Heinz 57 Varieties.

Additional Examples of Individuals Who Had Character:

James' first, entrepreneurial experience was owning the butcher shop in his hometown. To get the business of the local hotel, he was required to buy a bottle of liquor for the head cook each week. James did not smoke or drink, so he refused to pay the bribe to do business with the hotel. Consequently, his butcher business failed. Later, he would say, "I lost everything that I had, but I learned never to compromise." By sticking to his morals, he opened another store called the "Golden Rule." Eventually, James Cash Penney changed the name of the store to J.C. Penney.

William Jr. struggled in school. After being kicked out of school for the third time, his father had him come to work with him working 10 hours a day. Over time, he got married and he moved out on his own. He started his entrepreneur experience by selling umbrellas, newspapers, and gum. It wasn't until he was 32 years old when he had any success with chewing gum. Six years later, his competitors tried to put him out of business because he would not join an illegal, price-fixing cartel with them. When Wrigley was 46 years old, there was a serious economic depression, which put most people out of business, and which almost forced him into bankruptcy. Due to his character and reputation, he was able to secure a business loan for $250,000, which was almost twice his annual sales revenue. And, by putting the money into a national advertising campaign, within one year he went from $170,000 in sales revenue to $3 million in sales revenue. And, as they say, the rest is history.

How to Strengthen Your Character:

1. **Keep Your Word:** In Dr. Seuss's book, Horton Hatches the Egg, Horton the Elephant agrees to sit on a bird's nest, and the bird says she will be right back. The bird does not come back, and Horton continues to sit on the egg. When passerby would ask him what he was doing, his reply was resolute; he would say, "I meant what I said and I said what I meant; an elephant is faithful 100%." You should always endeavor to keep your word at all cost.

2. **Be Impeccably Honest:** When you think of someone's reputation, you usually think first of his or her honesty. George Washington wrote, "I hope I shall always possess firmness and virtue enough to maintain what I consider the most enviable of all titles, the character of an honest man." When Abraham Lincoln was a store clerk, he discovered he had accidently shortchanged a customer by 6 cents. Most people would have just written it off as no big deal. However, that night he closed the store, and he walked the 3 miles to her door to

repay her for his mistake. Honesty is the root of character.

3. **Honor Your Time:** Imagine that there is a bank that credits your account each morning with $86,400, carries over no balance from day to day, allows you to keep no cash balance, and every evening cancels whatever part of the amount you had failed to use during the day. What would you do? Draw out every cent, of course! Well, everyone has such a bank. Its name is time. Every morning, it credits you with 86,400 seconds. Every night, it writes off, as lost, whatever of this you had failed to invest to good purpose. It carries over no balance. It allows no overdraft. The clock is running. Make the most of today.

4. **Stand Up for Your Beliefs:** In 1849, Harriet Tubman and her brothers ran away after their master had died. However, her brothers became scared and returned to the plantation. In complete isolation, she followed the North Star to freedom in Pennsylvania. She made a vow that she would help her family and friends win their freedom, as well. As for her family,

Harriet successfully rescued her sister in 1850, one brother in 1851, her other three brothers in 1854, and her parents in 1857.

William Still (who recorded activities of the Underground Railroad) described Tubman as: "A woman of no pretensions, indeed, a more ordinary specimen of humanity could hardly be found among the most unfortunate-looking farmhands of the South. Yet, in point of courage, shrewdness and disinterested exertions to rescue her fellow-men... she was without her equal."

5. **Respect Others:** While interviewing Bill Bartmann, he told me that at the age of 14 he had been homeless for a period of time. This caused him to drop out of high school, and to join a gang. When he was 17 years old, he worked in a hotel, and there was a woman in management who kept calling him a "bright young kid." After a month or two of this, he inquired why she called him that. She said that it was what the owner of the hotel had put on his application after his interview. This respect from

someone he admired as a businessman completely changed his outlook on himself. It inspired him to get his GED, put himself through college and law school, and eventually build his own company to a billion dollar empire. At one point, he was ranked as one of the 25 Richest People in America by Forbes. Bill told me that none of this would have happened if the owner of the hotel had not recognized him as the "bright young kid."

Conclusion

I once heard a quote that seems to ring true, "Poor people have big TVs, and rich people have big libraries." If you want to change your circumstances, then you will need to change your belief system. You should hunger for truth and knowledge because it is at the root of every belief system. You were born to adapt and change. However, you should never look back. The past is where it is, you should leave it there. Prepare for tomorrow and you will be on your way to changing your life and leaving a legacy that future generations will be inspired by. I leave you with these inspiring words from Benjamin Franklin:

> "If you would not be forgotten, as soon as you are dead and rotten, either write things worth reading, or do things worth the writing."
> – Benjamin Franklin

About Woody Woodward

Woody Woodward is a bestselling author of 12 books on personal, relationship, and business strategy. His first book, Millionaire Dropouts – Inspiring Stories of the World's Greatest Failures, was a top 10 Forbes Book Club recommendation. For his latest book, Your Emotional Fingerprint: 7 Secrets That Will Transform Your Life, he spent 9 years studying 1,000 biographies as well as interviewing over 2,500 people from around the world to discover what drives human behavior and how an individual can take personal responsibility to produce a targeted result. The Emotional Fingerprint technique was presented to the United Nations to assist them with reaching their millennial goals. He has shared his cutting edge techniques on ABC, CBS, NBC, and FOX.

Before Mr. Woodward was an author and success strategist, he ran multiple companies. As a perpetual entrepreneur and product developer, he studied the influence of persuasion in regards to buying habits, decision-making, and product loyalty. He has worked with NASCAR, NBL, NBA, NHL, NFL, Warner Music, Sony, Disney, and BMG. His products have sold in Wal-Mart, Toys R Us, Sears, JC Penney's, and QVC. He currently consults for many public and private companies.

Websites:

www.NoMoreTherapy.com

www.InspireTheHellOutOfYou.com

www.ConnectToProfit.com

www.MeetWoody.com

To contact Mr. Woodward for a speaking engagement or strategy session email him at: Woody@MeetWoody.com